1 MONTH OF FREE READING

at

www.ForgottenBooks.com

By purchasing this book you are eligible for one month membership to ForgottenBooks.com, giving you unlimited access to our entire collection of over 1,000,000 titles via our web site and mobile apps.

To claim your free month visit: www.forgottenbooks.com/free726576

* Offer is valid for 45 days from date of purchase. Terms and conditions apply.

ISBN 978-0-484-42665-7
PIBN 10726576

This book is a reproduction of an important historical work. Forgotten Books uses
state-of-the-art technology to digitally reconstruct the work, preserving the original format
whilst repairing imperfections present in the aged copy. In rare cases, an imperfection in
the original, such as a blemish or missing page, may be replicated in our edition. We do,
however, repair the vast majority of imperfections successfully; any imperfections that
remain are intentionally left to preserve the state of such historical works.

Forgotten Books is a registered trademark of FB &c Ltd.
Copyright © 2018 FB &c Ltd.
FB &c Ltd, Dalton House, 60 Windsor Avenue, London, SW19 2RR.
Company number 08720141. Registered in England and Wales.

For support please visit www.forgottenbooks.com

TWENTY-NINTH ANNUAL REPORT OF THE

BOARD OF TRUSTEES

AND

TWENTY-EIGHTH ANNUAL REPORT OF THE

LIBRARIAN OF THE PUBLIC LIBRARY OF THE DISTRICT OF COLUMBIA

FOR THE FISCAL YEAR
ENDED JUNE 30

1926

**WASHINGTON
GOVERNMENT PRINTING OFFICE
1926**

BOARD OF TRUSTEES

CHARLES J. BELL, term expires 1928.
THEODORE W. NOYES, term expires 1928.
WENDELL P. STAFFORD, term expires 1928.
FRANK W. BALLOU, term expires 1930.
ALBERT J. BERRES, term expires 1930.
JOHN B. LARNER, term expires 1930.
Mrs. MARIE MANNING GASCH, term expires 1932.
MAURICE OTTERBACK, term expires 1932.
Mrs. LYMAN B. SWORMSTEDT, term expires 1932.

OFFICERS OF THE BOARD

THEODORE W. NOYES, *president*.[1]
WENDELL P. STAFFORD, *vice president*.
JOHN B. LARNER, *secretary*.
GEORGE F. BOWERMAN, *librarian, treasurer, and assistant secretary*.

STANDING COMMITTEES

BOOKS

JOHN B. LARNER, *chairman*.
WENDELL P. STAFFORD.
Mrs. MARIE MANNING GASCH.

BUILDING

MAURICE OTTERBACK, *chairman*.
WENDELL P. STAFFORD.
Mrs. LYMAN B. SWORMSTEDT.

EMPLOYEES

WENDELL P. STAFFORD, *chairman*.
Mrs. MARIE MANNING GASCH.
FRANK W. BALLOU.

FINANCE

CHARLES J. BELL, *chairman*.
JOHN B. LARNER.
ALBERT J. BERRES.

RULES

FRANK W. BALLOU, *chairman*.
JOHN B. LARNER.
MAURICE OTTERBACK.

BOOKBINDING, ETC.

Mrs. MARIE MANNING GASCH, *chairman*.
MAURICE OTTERBACK.
FRANK W. BALLOU.

SPECIAL COMMITTEES

LEGISLATION

ALBERT J. BERRES, *chairman*.
Mrs. LYMAN B. SWORMSTEDT.
MAURICE OTTERBACK.

DONATIONS

Mrs. LYMAN B. SWORMSTEDT, *chairman*.
CHARLES J. BELL.
ALBERT J. BERRES.

BRANCH LIBRARIES

CHARLES J. BELL, *chairman*.
FRANK W. BALLOU.
MAURICE OTTERBACK.

---

[1] The president is ex officio a member of all committees.

REPORT OF THE BOARD OF TRUSTEES OF THE PUBLIC LIBRARY

WASHINGTON, *September 23, 1926.*
THE COMMISSIONERS OF THE DISTRICT OF COLUMBIA:

In accordance with law the library trustees present herewith their report for the fiscal year 1926. It consists of a detailed report to the trustees by the librarian together with certain comments of their own on the year's progress and the steps necessary in their estimation to build up in the District of Columbia a public library system required by the population of Washington and commensurate with the importance of the seat of the National Government.

IMPORTANCE OF LIBRARY SERVICE

America prides itself upon its public educational system. The welfare and importance of the schools have long occupied the attention of all thoughtful persons, but less consideration has been given to public libraries. Now, however, they have become recognized as an indispensable part of the educational service essential for the diffusion of knowledge on which in no small measure the prosperity and advancement of the community depend. The growing emphasis on adult education has made library service vital.

WASHINGTON'S PUBLIC LIBRARY FACILITIES

Washington is still a long way from supplying the community with adequate library facilities. An overcrowded central library, three branches in separate buildings, and two subbranches in the Chevy Chase and Tenley public-school buildings are not sufficient to furnish library service easily accessible to the homes and offices of all residents of Washington.

BRANCH DEVELOPMENT DEMANDED BY LIBRARY LAW

Nation-wide statistics demonstrate that the use of libraries depends directly upon the number of branches and their accessibility. The trustees note with satisfaction that this fundamental point is fully recognized by Congress in the amended organic law in the words:

Said library shall consist of a central library and such number of branch libraries so located and so supported as to furnish books and other printed matter and information service convenient to the homes and offices of all residents of the said District.

The fact that this matter is specifically covered in the law would seem to indicate congressional approval of more rapid development of branches and marks in the opinion of the trustees definite and most encouraging progress.

THE PROBLEM OF LIBRARY SITES

The matter of suitable library sites in view of the rapid growth of Washington has been giving the trustees increasing concern. They welcome therefore the inclusion of the Public Library in the amended National Capital Park and Planning Commission law, which assures consideration of the subject by that commission.

LIBRARY LEGISLATION AND APPROPRIATIONS

The library was most fortunate in the consideration given to its needs both by the Budget Bureau and by the District of Columbia and Appropriation Committees of the Senate and House, with the following results: (1) The amended organic law provides explicitly rather than by implication for a thoroughly modern library system. (2) The appropriation for 1927 was increased by $34,200 over that for 1926 and included an item of $20,000 to be applied to much needed renovation of the central library and Takoma Park branch buildings. It also provides for the establishment of two subbranches in public-school buildings. The report of the House committee included a statement to the effect that "the committee is convinced that the library is handicapped in the performance of its mission through the inadequacy of its staff." (3) A deficiency appropriation permitted the opening (though on a limited schedule only) of the Mount Pleasant children's room in March. These gains are substantial marks of recognition by Congress of the library's value and it is hoped, precursors of its more rapid development. The provision requiring the reversion to the United States Treasury of the desk fund (money collected from the loss and overdetention of books) provided in the new law to take effect at the end of the current fiscal year was enacted solely in accordance with good budgetary practice.

THE YEAR'S RECORD OF SERVICE

Larger appropriations are only justified by expanding service and the trustees point with pride to the growth in library use. The home circulation of books totaled 1,298,405 volumes, an increase of 205,872 volumes over 1925. Although no methods are possible which measure accurately the reference and advisory service of a library, it is generally considered that they increase in proportion to the increases in circulation. The use of the reading rooms by students, the growing requests by individuals for reading lists, the gratifying use of the biography room opened during the year, the increased number of telephone calls for specific information, bear out this theory and are witnesses to the enlarging use of the library.

THE NEXT STEPS

Last year the trustees presented in their report a five-year program of library development. They trust that this program may be carried on rapidly. The immediate steps which they hope may be made possible by the appropriations for the fiscal year 1928 are: (a) Increases in staff, book collection and maintenance which will bring the present organization up to standard and will provide for the opening of the children's room of the Mount Pleasant branch the normal number of hours (approximately $38,560, bringing the total for the present establishment to $309,860); (b) eight additional library branches in public-school buildings (approximately $7,650 for each, a total of $62,250); (c) a branch in a rented building in the Rhode Island Avenue section ($9,150); (d) provision for the site for a branch in the northeastern section of the city as a start toward the next step in branch building (approximately $15,000)— a grand total of $396,260.

There is also a growing demand on the part of citizens that the central library and branches should be kept opened until 9 p. m. every Wednesday instead of closing at 3 p. m. as has been necessitated by lack of sufficient staff for the past several years. The trustees hope that this condition may speedily be remedied. Provision for longer hours on Sundays and holidays would also permit the library to render a real service to workers at hours which would be most convenient to them.

The trustees desire to express their appreciation of the consideration given to library problems by the commissioners.

In the absence of President Theodore W. Noyes, I have the honor to offer this report on behalf of the Board of Library Trustees.

Respectfully submitted.

WENDELL P. STAFFORD,
Vice President Library Trustees.

REPORT OF THE LIBRARIAN

WASHINGTON, *July 31, 1926.*

LADIES AND GENTLEMEN: I have the honor to submit herewith my report on the work of the Public Library for the fiscal year ended June 30, 1926.

This report consists of abridgments of the reports to me by chiefs of divisions of the library service and of my comments on matters of general library administration.

The most important statistical facts of the library's resources, services rendered, and its finances are summarized in a table arranged according to the American Library Association's approved form (pp. 17–18).

The table of municipal library expenditures, book circulations and branch-library provision in American cities above 200,000 population, as compared with Washington, has its usual place in the report (p. 19). Although these tables have since 1911 been compiled for the purpose of answering questions raised at hearings before congressional appropriation committees, their utility has been widely recognized. For example, the table published a year ago has been reprinted by the World Almanac, the American City, School and Society, the Library Journal, and the Publishers' Weekly. The Louisville Free Public Library (as in some earlier years) reprinted it in rearranged form as the basis of its campaign for an increased budget.

The treasurer's report, covering the funds under the supervision of the library trustees, will be found on pages 19–21.

THE PROGRESS OF THE YEAR

The library progress of the past year is best shown by the following significant events, some of which will have fuller treatment elsewhere in this report:

1. The enactment of the amendments to the library's organic law by which the library has a new charter for progress. (Discussion on pp. 14–15; amended law printed in full on pages 22–23.)

2. The library also found a place in the amended National Capital Park and Planning Commission law by which the question of library sites will have consideration by this commission to the library's advantage in the building of branch libraries. (Extract from law on p. 24.)

3. An appropriation in a deficiency bill for the opening in March of the Mount Pleasant branch library children's room, which because of lack of staff had not yet been opened.

4. An increase in appropriations for the coming fiscal year of $34,200 over 1926, including increases for personnel, Sunday and holiday opening, binding, and a much-needed item of $20,000 for

repairs to buildings and equipment. This increase was accompanied by a statement in the report of the House Committee on Appropriations saying that "The committee is convinced that the library is handicapped in the performance of its mission through the inadequacy of its staff." Such conviction should and probably will lead to still further increases later.

5. The appropriation for the coming year included provision for a branch librarian to operate subbranches at the public schools at Chevy Chase and Tenleytown. These subbranches will be opened on alternate days. Although the appropriation is very inadequate, the principle of maintaining branches of the Public Library in public schools is established in fact as well as in the newly amended library law.

6. The library circulated into Washington homes and offices 1,298,405 volumes and 118,426 mounted pictures, or 1,416,831 pieces; as compared with a total of 1,205,186 pieces in the previous year, consisting of 1,092,533 volumes and 112,653 mounted pictures. The library's large and constantly growing reference and advisory work can not be expressed by statistics; some of these services are summarized in the succeeding departmental reports.

THE DELAYS OF THE YEAR

Contrasted with the events that mark the advances of the year are the negative factors that mark the halts on the road of library progress. Among them may be mentioned the following:

1. The continued closing of the central library and of all branches every Wednesday at 3 p. m. and every Saturday afternoon in summer. Lack of staff has compelled this action for several years, and it must be continued until the force is enlarged. It is annoying to readers who forget and by no means creditable to the Public Library of the National Capital. It is hoped that a further increase in personnel another year will make it possible to keep the library open the hours customarily maintained by public libraries, 9 a. m. to 9 p. m., on all week days.

2. The Mount Pleasant branch library children's room, though no longer closed, is open only on a reduced schedule, because the staff is insufficient. Estimates for a larger staff will be pressed for next year.

3. Although the principle of conducting branch libraries in school buildings is established by the maintenance by the Public Library of subbranches the coming year in the E. V. Brown and Janney Schools, the beginning is a pitifully small one as compared with the need and the opportunity. It is particularly disappointing that it has never been possible to open a branch library in the Eastern High School, where a fine large room, all fitted up with library furniture and designed from the beginning for a branch of the Public Library, has been standing idle and unused for three or four years for lack of appropriations for book stock and service there. The school authorities have long been ready and willing to have a branch library there, as well as branches in several other schools, including the Armstrong Manual Training High School and most of the new junior high schools, but the proposals for such service included in library trustees' estimates have never materialized in appropriations.

CIRCULATION AND ADVISORY SERVICE

The registration statistics show that 23,283 applicants were registered during the year, so that the total number of cards in force is 63,967, an increase of 3,800. Special privilege cards were issued to 450 teachers, so that the total is 1,363; 182 strangers availed themselves of the use of the library by making deposits of $5 each. The volumes lent for home use numbered 1,298,405. The circulation administered by the adult circulation department (including branches, high schools, stations, etc.) numbered 641,390 volumes and 118,426 mounted pictures.

That the opportunities for continued education, social betterment, and business profit which are offered by the library are becoming more vital to the community is shown by the number of persons turning to the library with their problems and by their apparent trust that they will receive authoritative material. In order that the books may prove to be not merely commodities, but points of contact in thought and action, special attention was paid to the needs of each applicant seeking aid through an enlarged advisory service, with the advisers specializing in particular fields. The opening of a new division of biography still further showed the advantage of open over closed shelves and afforded free access to biographical material in charge of persons conversant with that literature. As the biography room adjoins the fiction room, it has been observed that many fiction readers have taken to reading biography. (From the report of Grace B. Finney, chief circulation department.)

BRANCH LIBRARY SERVICE

Takoma Park.—The varied community interests are reflected in the 128 meetings held at the branch, with an attendance of 4,096 persons. The flower shows arranged by the Horticultural Club have attracted many visitors, among whom have been some distinguished horticulturists. This club has been very generous in presenting to the branch a number of attractive books on gardening. The club is also making plans for beautifying the library grounds, and has voted $100 for the purpose. Several periodicals given by the home and school association increase the usefulness of that part of the branch collection. The editor of the Takoma News has continued his generous allowance of space for library items. The book collection numbers 9,510 volumes. The circulation of 55,275 volumes was an increase of 3,912. With the erection of many dwellings and apartment houses in the vicinity now going on, the Takoma branch hopes for a larger growth during the coming year.

Southeastern.—In spite of too small a staff and too few books, the branch has successfully shouldered a total circulation of 137,559 volumes, an increase of 8,242 over that of the previous year. Perhaps much of this growth is due to the greater use of the branch by high-school students. During its three and one-half years, the branch has established a friendly acquaintance with its clientele. To determine how much of the community and what sections are registered, a thorough checking of the registration file with the city street directory has been made. This shows a satisfactory representation of the southeast as well as much of the northeast, since that section does not yet have its own branch. The branch book collection now numbers more than 11,000 volumes. The adult collection needs developing along certain subjects; the juvenile collection needs almost a complete replenishing.

Mount Pleasant.—The bus and trolley lines in the immediate neighborhood and the size of the adult department have tended to make the branch take on many of the features of a regional branch library. Regular adult borrowers who live over 3 miles away—in Chevy Chase, Cleveland Park, and Georgetown—are frequent users. At the end of the first full year of adult work (May 16, 1925–May 15, 1926) the adult circulation reached 151,000. In March the girls' and boys' room, which had been equipped and stocked for several months, opened its doors with a staff of five and service to the public 20 hours weekly. The circulation since opening has averaged 8,000 books a month. In addition to the customary advisory work, the branch's floor assistants have striven to popularize the use of lists and bibliographies. During the year 858 adults have availed themselves of lists on their individual interests and problems. Six lessons on the use of the library were given to 135 pupils of the Powell Junior High School. Two McFarland Junior High School classes also had one hour each of directed library study. The auditorium of the branch was used 165 times. The book collection of the branch is about 35,000 volumes, about equally divided between adult and juvenile collections. The home circulation for the year was 189,730 volumes, 154,770 adult and 34,960 juvenile; the latter represent the three and one-half months during which the children's room was open.

(From the reports of the branch librarians: Rebecca P. Warner, Takoma Park; Frances S. Osborne, Southeastern; Margery Quigley, Mount Pleasant.)

DEPOSIT STATIONS AND HIGH SCHOOLS

The stations and high-schools division reports a circulation of 74,650 volumes. There were 8,267 books sent to 11 deposit stations and 19 public and parochial schools, normal schools, and colleges. The high-school librarians circulated 40,600 volumes, an increase of 1,143, and used for reference 6,872 volumes. The crowded conditions prevailing at several high schools prevented greater orders for books needed for reference, since requests had to be limited to books required for a particular time. The educational directors of the several department stores endeavored to develop the knowledge of the employees in their particular lines of work. A clerk who did intensive reading on the manufacture of silk, its history, etc., would become an expert. The loss in station circulation was partly due to the death of the capable librarian of one of the larger stations. The library station conducted by the pastor of a colored church in connection with his social community work was discontinued after years of usefulness. The work became too strenuous without the aid of an assistant. The loss of this station was counterbalanced by the addition of two new parochial high schools and an active exchange of books at the Americanization school.

The library station conducted at the E. V. Brown School, Chevy Chase, and maintained for several years by the Chevy Chase Citizens' and Home and Schools Associations becomes next year a subbranch by an appropriation from Congress. The services of the former trained librarian, who did excellent work under adverse circumstances, will be retained. (From the report of Cornelia S. Charles, supervisor of stations and high schools.)

REFERENCE DEPARTMENT

The work of the reference department, including the reference room and industrial division at the main library and the reference service of the branches, has been kept up to a high standard. In the reference room the service is general in character, covering all except scientific, technical, and business subjects, which are the special field of the industrial division; the reference work of the branches is largely with high-school students. The director of reference work has had general supervision of the work of the industrial division, including book selection and promotion of plans for improvement and extension; has prepared the periodical subscription list for the library in consultation with heads of departments and branch librarians, and has visited branches to examine reference collections and to confer with branch librarians. Staff meetings were held for all members of the library staff doing reference and information work. The director of reference work was chairman of a committee on bibliography, which submitted a detailed report on ideals and methods of bibliographical work in this library, adopted as a basis for such work in the future.

Reference service covering a wide variety of subjects has been extended to persons coming to the central reference room and by telephone. The number of questions recorded was 9,613, including 1,005 telephone calls, which shows a large increase in the use of the telephone. A few representative questions are: The source of the saying "the battle of Waterloo was won on the playing fields of Eton"; where was the press of John Dunlap, the printer for the First Continental Congress; all the definitions of Castile soap which can be found; what commercial treaties has the United States made with China. The use of the Washingtoniana collection is increasing, which shows that the value of this unique and well arranged collection of local material is being more and more recognized. From this source have been answered such questions as: The location of Fort Carroll on the Potomac; material on the history of the District of Columbia National Guard; early Washington schools. The most important bibliographical work accomplished during the year was the list on American artists represented at the tenth exhibition of American paintings, held at the Corcoran Gallery. (From the report of Emma Hance, director of reference work.)

INDUSTRIAL DIVISION

The outstanding features of the year were the making of a survey of activities and the participation in the second annual industrial exposition sponsored by the Washington Chamber of Commerce. The survey revealed the actual happenings for three consecutive weeks during January and showed an average weekly attendance of 1,600 persons and 300 questions answered. The number of persons visiting the room was twice the circulation figures. The occupations of the users of the room rank as follows: 1, government clerks; 2, students; 3, business men; 4, no occupation; 5, professional men, including teachers; 6, tradespeople.

By far the biggest forward step of the division since its establishment was the participation in the industrial exposition. The publicity for the entire library was large. The fact that the library should be represented at such an exhibition made quite as much impression as did the exhibit of books and pictures on industrial subjects. Six annotated lists on advertising, real estate, books for the home maker, engineering, building construction, and business organization and management were prepared and distributed. The exhibit included trade catalogues, house organs, and books relating to local industries. The collection of 100 popular books in science recommended by the Washington Academy of Sciences attracted general attention. Registration slips were given out from the booth, thus making a direct contact with new readers. (From the report of Ruth H. Todd, chief, industrial division.)

CHILDREN'S DEPARTMENT

The juvenile circulation, exclusive of the traveling libraries division, was 620,494 volumes, a gain of 83,588 or 15½ per cent over the previous year. This work was carried on in the schools division and four children's rooms, each of which showed an increase.

Besides the reference, circulation, and clerical work that this represents it has back of it a heavy amount of book reviewing, book ordering, bibliographical work, and interviews with adults seeking advice. Each book used in the system is carefully read and a book note is made giving a critical evaluation of it, a comparison between the new book and others on the same subject, and, in the case of tales, something of the story. Thus the library is assured of the quality of the books read by the children, no matter where in the system they are secured.

The outstanding event of the year was the opening of the children's room at the Mount Pleasant branch. It is interesting to find that 84 per cent of the children registered in the room are new users of the library. This demonstrates the need, in this day of congested traffic, of branches within easy reach of the children in various neighborhoods. All of the large cities and most of the small ones have such branch systems. It is hard to face the fact that Washington is not caring for its children in any such way. Each section of the city should have its library and each child his friendly "library teacher" to aid him.

It is gratifying to report three generous gifts to the library children. In December the Governor Thomas Welles Chapter of the Children of the American Revolution presented to the central children's room a beautiful silk American flag. This flag adds greatly to the appearance of the room and the pleasure of the children and staff. In June the Richard Lord Jones Chapter of the Children of the American Revolution presented to the girls' and boys' room at Mount Pleasant branch a silk American flag. The new room is festive with this appreciated gift.

The Parent-Teachers' Association of the Powell, Johnson, and Bancroft schools gave to the girls' and boys' room of the Mount Pleasant branch money to have two attractive reading lists made. Since war time the library has not had money for printed lists for distribution. They are most important in improving the reading taste of children and are helpful to parents as suggestions. (From the report of Louise P. Latimer, director, work with children.)

SCHOOLS DIVISION

One of the outstanding assets of the library of to-day, and perhaps its greatest contribution to young people, is its capacity for fostering literary appreciation by inculcating a joy in books. The contribution of the schools division to such an objective is mirrored in its circulation figures which reach a total of 322,594 volumes; 1,882 collections were sent into 679 classrooms in 151 schools. This circulation is the largest in the history of the division; the increase over the preceding year is 27,108, or 9½ per cent.

It is effective cooperation with the schools which enables the library to send into classrooms carefully picked books in small numbers (one for each pupil) and to leave them for a two-month period for home circulation. This is not long enough for curiosity to be entirely allayed, but it is long enough for each child to discover the books which have an outstanding appeal for him. These books do not represent supplementary reading but reading which nevertheless takes advantage of interests aroused through the curriculum. They develop readers from nonreaders and serve to establish reading habits among those who like reading, but not enough to make the effort to secure books. With both groups the enthusiasm and encouragement of the teacher and the contagion of the children's liking of different books accomplish surprising results.

This classroom service does not rival the service of the children's rooms in libraries with their contribution of book atmosphere, opportunity for wider range of selection, and association with specialists in children's literature. With the children's rooms, however, they operate happily toward the end that children growing up may " when on their own " turn to books for pleasure. (From the report of M. Ethel Bubb, supervisor, work with schools.)

PICTURE DIVISION AND EXHIBITIONS

The picture division has shown progress in the circulation of 118,426 mounted pictures, an increase of 5,773 over the previous year. Sets were sent to 1,065 teachers in 173 public schools of all grades, private and Sunday schools, and four colleges. The work with individuals and clubs has greatly increased; 10 clubs were regular borrowers throughout the club season. The increased reference work with magazines, newspapers, and individuals, and for commercial use often made necessary searching to secure material for difficult problems; though some material was obscure, it was seldom unattainable.

The rapidly growing importance of visual aids in education is manifest. In many instances the teachers build their lessons about the pictures, using them as the basis of the project. The introduction of motion-picture and Trans-Lux machines in the schools has in no way interfered with the use of the "still" pictures, but, on the contrary, has increased their use through the greater opportunity they offer the teachers for analysis. An outline of the collection and work of the picture division was prepared to facilitate use by borrowers.

Attractive exhibits served as visual aids in focusing attention on special collections of books. The graphic arts division of the National Museum started two traveling exhibits at the library; one on the processes employed in print making, the other consisting of tools and material used in bookbinding. Garden and better-homes week was featured by a miniature colonial house and garden loaned by the Better Homes Association, and music week with curious old instruments loaned by the music division of the National Museum. Pictures of various industries formed the background for the industrial division's exhibit at the industrial exhibition sponsored by the Washington Chamber of Commerce. (From the report of Dorothy H. Stokes, in charge of picture collection and exhibits.)

ACCESSIONS—PURCHASES AND GIFTS

An increase of 7,767 accessions over the previous year shows that the order and accessions division has accomplished an unusual amount of work. There was an increased appropriation for the stocking of the Mount Pleasant branch children's room. The books were purchased and ready several months in advance of the opening of the room. The accessions numbered 34,189 volumes, of which 30,830 were purchased, at an average cost of $1.39. The withdrawals numbered 10,467 volumes. The net strength of the library collection at the close of the year was 295,217 volumes. The gifts of books included the annual gift of review copies of new books from the Evening Star and a collection of books for lenten reading presented by Mrs. W. C. Rives. The copyright transfers received from the Library of Congress numbered 1,751 volumes. Much free material, books and pamphlets, was secured, through requests, for the main library and for the three branches. (From the report of Edith W. Moore, chief, order and accessions division.)

CATALOGUE DEPARTMENT

The statistics submitted by the catalogue department show a notable increase in output of work. There were 33,100 volumes classified and catalogued; of these 4,155 were new titles and analytical entries made for books of composite authorship or treating of a variety of topics. About 15,000 books were catalogued for the children's room at the Mount Pleasant branch. Cataloguing for the branch libraries has substantially increased the departmental work. With the advent of more branches an additional cataloguer will be needed to make the rounds of all branches and care for the catalogue and shelf-list records.

A considerable amount of time was given to the further expansion of the Cutter classification. Many sociological and technological subjects required development. The automobile industry was expanded to 22 divisions and the separation of the engineering from the economic aspect of waterways was finished.

The soiled condition of the cards in the public catalogue presents a never-ending problem. All of the most unsightly sections have been rewritten and guide cards renewed; this has helped much to improve the general appearance of the catalogue. (From the report of Julia H. Laskey, chief of the catalogue department.)

BOOKBINDING

There were 8,919 volumes bound for the main library and branches; 2,066 current magazines were reinforced; and 15,376 other books, pamphlets, etc., handled as different types of work. Of the number bound, 3,299 were rebound by an outside binder. These books are shipped in well-lined book trunks furnished by the contractor.

Magazine binders were constructed for the thin publications assigned to the reference department. They are covered in full buckram, lined with White House cover paper and fastened by Cushman and Denison binder clips. A uniform stenciled paper title is added and the entire case given two coats of Barco for protection and sanitary considerations.

The experiment of purchasing new fiction, replacements, and juveniles in reinforced binding has been given a thorough trial. Except as an emergency measure to tide over a period when rebinding could not be handled and to keep in constant use the collection at a new branch the use of reinforced bindings has not been found economical. Active circulation in a large library reduces such reinforced bindings to a condition where the books are too disreputable to remain on the shelves but are nevertheless entirely too valuable to discard, so that they must be rebound. (From the report of Elizabeth P. Gray, curator of collection and supervisor of binding.)

THE STAFF—TRAINING AND CLASSIFICATION

For 20 years previous to the past year the library conducted an annual class during six to eight months for discovering and training candidates eligible for appointment to junior positions in the library. Heads of departments of the library service gave the instruction and supervised the practice work of the students. The plan worked well, but had become increasingly burdensome. Furthermore, library salaries under the operation of the classification act of 1923 had so improved as to justify requiring candidates for junior positions to secure their technical instruction at their own expense. When last year the George Washington University revived some of its courses of instruction in library science, interrupted more than 20 years ago, the library discontinued its training class and referred applicants to the university. Eligible members of the university's classes in library science who wished to be considered for junior positions in the Public Library were accepted for supervised practice work. Inasmuch as many of the candidates were pursuing other regular academic subjects toward a bachelor's degree, this plan, which relieves the library from giving the technical instruction but enables it to test the fitness of the students for appointment, seems to be working well and will be continued.

The operation of the classification act of 1923 as applied to the library service continues to show progressive improvement. Previous reports have recorded that the junior and intermediate staff quite generally and some of the higher positions had been properly allocated. During the past year appeals for higher allocations were granted in the case of two additional intermediate positions, but also, fortunately, in the case of the following higher positions: Chief, circulation department; chief, catalogue department; branch librarian, southeastern branch; and the librarian's secretary (chief clerk). There still remain to be corrected the allocations of a few more chiefs of major and minor departments and divisions and their immediate subordinates, particularly the director of reference work and her principal assistants. This is also true of the positions of chief librarian and of assistant librarian, which are still one grade below what they should be.

The small amount of the appropriation granted for increments last year was nearly all absorbed by the reallocation of positions to higher grades at advanced salaries, so that it was possible to allow increments to the salaries of only a few members of the staff, although the efficiency ratings of practically all entitled them to such increments. Increments were granted to one employee on July 1, 1925, and to 14 on January 1, 1926; and at the beginning of the current year to 15 more.

From a total staff of 144 (exclusive of 5 in the bindery, but inclusive of employments from the desk fund and on the temporary roll) there were 40 resignations; 16 from the professional, nonprofessional, and clerical staff; 14 from the messenger and page force; and 10 from the building force. The turnover was therefore 28 per cent.

A fine spirit of service pervades the staff. Faithfulness, intelligence, and a desire for professional improvement are everywhere in evidence.

The librarian attended the midwinter meeting of the council of the American Library Association. Many members of the staff attended the joint conferences of the District of Columbia, Maryland, and Virginia library associations at Annapolis in October, 1925, and at Washington in May. The librarian has continued his service as chairman of the committee on civil-service relations of the American

Among the numerous contributions to professional literature by members of the library staff the following may be mentioned: "The free public library; its possibilities as a public-service agency," in the American Federationist for May, and "Municipal school and library expenditures" in School and Society for June 19—both by the librarian; "Simple notes on the use of books," by Miss Herbert, American Federationist for July, 1926; "A review of the Winnetka graded book list," by Louise P. Latimer, director of children's work (and several others engaged in library work for children), in Libraries for April and in Library Journal for April 1; "À bas jealousy!" in Publishers' Weekly for June 26, and a chapter on "Books for everybody" in the Asheville, N. C., Moonlight School Reader—both by Margery Quigley; and "After the sermon—what?" by Mary E. Clark in the spring book number of The Continent.

THE NEW LIBRARY LAW

The most promising event of the year for the future progress of the library was the enactment of important amendments to the library's organic act, originally passed 30 years ago and long in need of being brought up to date. Although the old law was fundamentally sound and did contain the progressive feature declaring the library to be "a supplement of the public educational system," it contained no mention of branch libraries. This and other lacks were no doubt partly responsible for the difficulty always experienced in securing appropriations for developing a modern public-library system for Washington. The first and most important amendment provides that—

said library shall consist of a central library and such number of branch libraries so located and so supported as to furnish books and other printed matter and information service convenient to the homes and offices of all residents of the said District.

The foregoing language and all of the discussion in and out of Congress leading up to the enactment of the amended law were to the effect that the Public Library is at present undersupported and underdeveloped as compared both with the needs of the population of Washington and with other progressive cities and that the intent of the law is to pave the way for speedily developing the Public Library's resources and service. It is therefore not unreasonable to expect that the enactment of this law will be speedily followed by the appropriations needed to make it come true.

The program for library development has for several years included the establishment of branch libraries in certain suburban school buildings, but nothing tangible toward that end had happened, perhaps because there had been no specific legislative authority therefor. Such authority is now given by an amendment to the law. Another amendment authorizes the library trustees "to rent suitable buildings or parts of buildings for use as branch libraries and distributing stations." This is intended to provide for branches in sections where suburban schools are overcrowded but whose populations do not yet justify separate branch libraries.

Another amendment specifically authorizes the previous practice of lending books without fees to residents of Maryland and Virginia—mostly Government employees—who have regular business or employment or attend school in the District. The amended law also authorizes the trustees to lend books to other residents of adjacent counties of Maryland and Virginia for fees. Such fees have been fixed at $3 per annum.

The amended law also gives specific authority to the District Commissioners to include in their estimates for appropriations " such sums as they may deem necessary for the proper maintenance of said library, including branches, for the purchase of land for sites for library buildings, and for the erection and enlargement of necessary library buildings." This is an important provision legislatively.

A new and unsought amendment of the law over which there is no great enthusiasm is one providing that after June 30, 1927, all receipts from fines and penalties shall be paid into the United States Treasury to the credit of the District. These receipts for the last year exceeded $15,000 and for the coming year are likely to equal or exceed $16,000; they also mean flexibility of expenditure for library purposes. The avowed purpose of the amendment was not, however, to cripple the library, but only in the interest of good budgetary practice. It is hoped and expected that Congress will not only take account of such collections and make them up by appropriations, but will also enable the library to go on doing the things it needs to do in the public interest without too many restrictions.

Precedent to the introduction of the library bill, many local organizations were addressed and their indorsements secured. This was followed by hearings before District committees of the Senate and House and personal interviews with many Senators and Members. The interest aroused by these efforts for the amended law also reacted helpfully for increased appropriations. One of the obstacles to be overcome has too often been the thought in Congress that since the Library of Congress supplies the library needs of the personnel of Congress and their families, it also meets the library needs of many others, and that therefore there is less occasion for large appropriations for a public library in Washington. Of great help to meet that mistaken thought has been a letter from the Librarian of Congress differentiating between the functions of the Library of Congress and of the Public Library and stressing the needs of the latter. That letter was printed in both Senate and House reports on the amended library law and in the hearings before the House Committee on Appropriations on the 1927 District of Columbia appropriation bill. It is also reprinted on page 24.

The amended organic law broadens the scope of the library and gives it a new charter of liberty and progress. The library needs many more branches and much larger appropriations to give the more than half million of people of Washington the library service they need. The machinery is now provided in the law. The Bureau of the Budget and the Appropriations Committees have evidenced an attitude of sympathy and helpfulness. The prospects, therefore, seem good that the appropriations needed will be forthcoming. (For text of law see pp. 22–23.)

ANNUAL ESTIMATES FOR FISCAL YEAR 1928

The library's appropriation for the fiscal year 1927 totals $271,300. Including the expected desk-fund collections of nearly or quite $16,000, the funds available for expenditure will during the current fiscal year probably exceed $287,000. Inasmuch as the desk-fund collections must, in accordance with law, after June 30, 1927, be deposited in the Treasury to the credit of the District and will not be available for expenditure by the library until appropriated by Congress, the appropriations for 1928 should include a compensatory sum. The estimates for 1928 as approved by the library trustees and filed with the District Commissioners total $396,260. This is $109,000 more than the combined 1927 appropriation and the expected desk-fund collections. These estimates (summary on p. 22) are designed (1) to bring the present organization, the central library and branches, up to a higher standard of efficiency; (2) to initiate new projects, including eight new branches in school buildings and one branch in rented quarters; and (3) to provide for the purchase of a site for the proposed northeastern branch library.

The estimate of $396,200 is modest as compared with the revenues of the municipal libraries of other large and progressive cities. The Census Bureau's estimate of the population of Washington on July 1, 1926, was 528,000. It is therefore an eminently conservative estimate that for the fiscal year 1927–28 Washington's population will be not less than 500,000. If the library trustees' estimates are appropriated entire, they would represent a per capita expenditure for the library of only 79.2 cents, as compared with the minimum standard of the American Library Association of $1 per capita, and as compared with several other large cities above $1, including Cleveland $1.39 and Boston $1.24.

The library trustees in filing their estimates with the District Commissioners gave it as their opinion that not to propose the estimates needed to take the forward steps contemplated by such estimates would represent failure on their part to put forward plans to give effect to the will of Congress as expressed in the amended library law.

It has so often been necessary to use in these annual reports the words "discouraging," "mark time," and similar pessimistic expressions accurately to describe rather persistent conditions, that it is now a pleasure to be able to use more optimistic words such as "progress," "forward steps," and the like. Although the library situation leaves much to be desired and there is still a long way to go before Washington's public library will be what it should be, yet on the whole the past year's record has been one of considerable progress for which there is reason for satisfaction. In closing my twenty-second annual report I wish to renew my thanks to the board of trustees for their confidence and support.

Respectfully submitted.

GEORGE F. BOWERMAN,
Librarian.

The TRUSTEES OF THE FREE PUBLIC LIBRARY.

APPENDIX TO LIBRARIAN'S REPORT

LIBRARY STATISTICS—AMERICAN LIBRARY ASSOCIATION FORM

ANNUAL REPORT FOR THE YEAR ENDED JUNE 30, 1926

Name of library: Public Library of the District of Columbia.
Population served: 513,994 (United States Census Bureau estimate for July 1, 1925).
Terms of use: Free for lending; free for reference.
Total number of agencies, 199.
Consisting of: Central library, 1; branches, 3 (in their own buildings); colleges, 3; schools, 170 (1,882 collections sent to 679 classrooms in 151 schools); stations, 11; home libraries, 0; playgrounds, 0; summer camps, 10; miscellaneous, 1.
Number of days open during the year (central library), 348 (closed all Wednesdays 3 p. m., Saturdays 1 p. m. July 1 through September 12, and Sundays and holidays July 1 through September 30).
Hours open each week for lending (central library), 66.
Hours open each week for reading (central library), 72 (Sundays and holidays open 2 to 6 p. m. October 1 through June 30).
Number of staff, 146; library service, 121; janitor service, 20; bookbinders, 5.
Total value of library property (exclusive of sites), $722,000.

Book stock and use

BOOK STOCK

Number of volumes at beginning of year	271,495
Number of volumes added during year:	
By purchase	30,830
By gift or exchange	3,097
By binding	262
Number of volumes lost or withdrawn	10,467
Total number at end of year	295,217
Of this number there are in reference department	21,708
Number of pamphlets received	4,692
Number of pictures, photographs, and prints added	2,350
Total number of pictures, photographs, and prints	61,607
Other additions (maps, 9; charts, 37)	46

Number of periodicals and newspapers currently secured: 814 titles, 1,053 copies, 7 newspapers.

Number of publications issued: Annual report, and 1 number of reference list; several miscellaneous.

USE OF COLLECTION

Number of volumes of fiction lent for home use (adult, 386,062; juvenile, 343,890)	729,952
Total number of volumes lent for home use (adult, 656,599; juvenile, 641,806)	1,298,405
Per cent fiction lent of total volumes lent (adult, 58; juvenile, 53)	56
Circulation per capita	2.53
Number of pictures, photographs, and prints lent for home use	118,426

Other circulation: Many clippings circulated, but no record kept.

Number of persons using library for reading and study: Large but not recorded.

REGISTRATION

Number of borrowers registered during year (adult, 16,454; juvenile, 6,625)	23,283
Total number of registered borrowers	63,967
Registration period, 3 years.	
Per cent registered borrowers of population served	12.4

Finance

Receipts from—	
Congressional appropriations	$237,569.60
State grants	
Invested funds	100.00
Membership fees	
Fines and sale of publications	11,775.03
Duplicate pay collection	1,851.17
Gifts	127.23
Interest on deposits	23.40
Other sources (if extraordinary, enumerate and state objects)	1,509.29
Unexpended balance from previous year	495.90
Grand total	253,451.62
Payments for maintenance:	
Library operating expenses—	
Librarians' salaries	161,823.26
Books	43,039.70
Periodicals	2,530.52
Binding	10,000.00
Supplies, stationery, printing, etc	2,607.20
Furniture, equipment, etc	121.18
Telephone, postage, freight, express	1,828.58
Other items	2,255.79
Total	224,206.23

Building maintenance expenses—

Janitors, mechanics, wages, etc	$16,540.00	
Cleaning supplies and equipment	1,552.06	
Building repairs and minor alterations	1,325.00	
Heat and light	6,186.73	
Other items	1,545.70	
Total		27,149.49
Total maintenance expenses		251,355.72
Maintenance expenditure per volume of circulation		$0.194
Maintenance expenditure per capita		.489

Municipal library expenditures and circulations per capita, 1925 or 1926

[Population figures used are the Census Bureau's estimates as of July 1, 1925; figures of expenditures circulations, and branch libraries furnished by the American Library Association or directly by the library]

Cities (ranked according to population)	Population (census estimate, July 1, 1925)	Expenditures 1925 or 1926 (exclusive of extraordinary expenses)	Per capita expenditures	Home circulation (volumes)	Expenditure per volume circulated	Per capita circulation (volumes)	Number of branches	Branches in separate buildings devoted exclusively to library purposes
New York City	5,873,356	$2,423,378.84	$0.413	16,944,905	$0.143	2.89	91	76
New York Public Library [1]	[2] 2,955,474	1,217,611.04	.412	9,018,339	.135	3.05	43	43
Brooklyn	[2] 2,203,235	913,522.00	.415	5,950,000	.154	2.70	28	23
Queens	[3] 714,647	292,245.80	.409	1,976,566	.148	2.76	20	10
Chicago	2,995,239	1,405,334.97	.469	11,002,736	.128	3.67	39	5
Philadelphia	1,979,364	634,514.70	.321	4,022,123	.158	2.03	29	29
Detroit	[3] 1,242,044	1,060,636.00	.854	4,105,744	.258	3.31	19	18
Los Angeles	[4] 1,125,000	850,176.84	.756	5,521,889	.154	4.91	45	21
Cleveland	936,485	1,306,347.17	1.39	6,287,331	.208	6.71	60	17
St. Louis	821,543	474,323.93	.577	2,746,914	.173	3.34	12	6
Baltimore	796,296	289,761.74	.364	1,004,061	.289	1.26	25	25
Boston	[2] 779,620	963,832.06	1.24	3,433,232	.281	4.40	31	10
Pittsburgh	631,563	574,916.76	.910	2,434,703	.236	3.86	10	9
Old city		481,590.07		1,915,465			9	8
Allegheny		93,326.69		519,238			1	1
Milwaukee [5]	599,647	346,317.47	.578	3,505,997	.099	5.85	13	3
San Francisco	557,530	273,047.54	.490	2,261,133	.121	4.06	11	11
Buffalo	[2] 538,016	279,627.63	.520	2,249,968	.124	4.18	10	5
Washington	513,994	251,355.72	.489	1,298,405	.194	2.53	3	3
Cincinnati [5]	512,341	375,145.73	.732	2,128,110	.176	4.15	28	11
Newark	452,513	332,041.47	.734	1,237,479	.268	2.73	5	5
Minneapolis	425,435	422,853.45	.994	2,304,728	.183	5.42	21	9
New Orleans	414,493	87,381.41	.211	685,191	.128	1.65	5	5
Kansas City	367,481	231,675.73	.630	1,501,607	.154	4.09	15	2
Indianapolis	358,819	343,706.72	.958	1,896,230	.181	5.28	19	12
Seattle	[4] 354,367	300,913.15	.849	2,312,181	.130	6.52	9	8
Portland [6]	[4] 351,760	310,460.46	.883	2,496,569	.124	7.10	17	12
Louisville [5]	342,400	164,688.78	.481	1,320,310	.125	3.86	15	9
Birmingham [6]	[4] 320,000	88,841.95	.278	648,247	.137	2.03	8	3
Rochester	[2] 316,786	183,956.29	.581	1,610,097	.114	5.08	10	3
Jersey City	315,280	200,619.13	.636	1,473,215	.136	4.67	8	3
Toledo	287,380	226,857.38	.789	1,381,770	.164	4.81	12	6
Denver	280,911	201,322.98	.717	1,435,230	.140	5.11	11	8
Columbus	279,836	74,410.00	.266	571,524	.130	2.04	0	0
Providence	[2] 267,918	247,866.04	.925	958,033	.259	3.58	7	1
Oakland	253,700	164,921.56	.650	1,114,245	.148	4.39	13	9
St. Paul	246,001	218,372.16	.888	1,504,998	.145	6.12	4	4
Omaha	211,768	89,451.74	.422	711,435	.126	3.36	4	2
Akron	[4] 210,000	49,605.10	.236	389,927	.127	1.86	3	1
Atlanta	[7] 200,616	95,110.00	.474	632,079	.150	3.15	8	4
Totals and means	26,159,502	15,543,772.60	.594	95,132,346	.163	3.64	{ 620 17.71	355 10.14 }
Medians			.630		.148	4.06		

[1] Circulation department only.
[2] State census, 1925.
[3] Special census, May 31, 1925.
[4] Estimate by librarian; no estimate by Census Bureau.
[5] City and county.
[6] City and county, exclusive of Bessemer and Fairfield, which have separate library systems; conditions abnormal; library largely destroyed by fire.
[7] 1920 census; no later estimate by Census Bureau.

REPORT OF TREASURER

[July 1, 1925 to June 30, 1926]

Receipts, desk fund:
  Balance on hand, June 30, 1925 _____ $378.36
  Fines—
    Issue department (central library) _____ $5,474.63
    Juvenile department (central library) _____ 1,648.39
    Industrial department (central library) _____ 733.56
    Takoma Park branch _____ 575.05
    Southeastern branch _____ 983.18
    Mount Pleasant branch _____ 2,145.77
    Stations _____ 88.05
        Total _____ 11,648.63

Receipts, desk fund—Continued.
Duplicate collection	$1,851.17
Reserves	187.71
Reissued cards	208.07
Books lost and injured	957.94
Catalogues sold	126.40
Sale of books	21.97
Nonresident fees	12.00
Check from Corcoran Gallery of Art for reference list	50.50
Interest on account	23.40
Total	15,466.15

Expenditures, desk fund:
Books	2,755.19
Services of assistants	8,263.26
Periodicals, subscriptions	675.50
Membership fees in learned societies	96.00
Reimbursing emergency fund	150.00
Post cards and stamps for overdue notices, etc	700.00
Traveling expenses	377.49
Auditing accounts	20.00
Premium on bond of treasurer	6.25
Fine computers (calendars)	4.00
Dodge car upkeep	181.36
A. L. A. lists "Reading with a purpose"	198.36
Printing	135.60
Miscellaneous	25.75
Total disbursements	13,588.76
Balance on hand, June 30, 1926	1,877.39
	15,466.15

Donation fund, including Henry Pastor memorial fund, Woman's Anthropological Society fund, and vending machine fund

GEORGE F. BOWERMAN, TREASURER, IN ACCOUNT WITH THE PUBLIC LIBRARY

Receipts:
To balance on hand, June 30, 1925	$117.54
Vending-machine fund	88.45
Woman's Anthropological Society fund	60.00
Henry Pastor memorial fund	40.00
Chevy Chase Station for books	20.23
G. H. Paine	21.70
Unclaimed deposits	5.00
Takoma Park Horticultural Club	9.80
Money found in building	28.15
Parent-Teachers' Association of Mount Pleasant section	25.00
Total	415.87

Expenditures:
Membership fees in learned societies	26.08
Periodical subscriptions	62.90
Books	76.63
Vending-machine supplies	31.75
To balance on hand, June 30, 1926	218.51
Total	415.87

The library is supported principally from Congressional appropriations, which are disbursed on pay rolls and vouchers audited by the District of Columbia auditor. A complete statement of library receipts and expenditures would therefore combine these appropriations with the funds controlled by the library trustees. Appropriations revert unless expended within the fiscal year, so that there are no balances from them to carry forward. The following summary combines receipts and expenditures from appropriations and from the desk and donation funds.

RECEIPTS

Congressional appropriations:
  Central library and branches—
Salaries, regular roll	$164,100.00
Salaries, Sunday and holiday roll	2,500.00
Salaries, employment of substitutes	3,500.00
Books and periodicals	42,000.00
Binding	10,000.00
Contingent expenses	15,000.00
Postage	370.00
Printing annual report	99.60
Total congressional appropriations	237,569.60

Desk fund:
Balance, June 30, 1925	378.36
Receipts, including interest	15,087.79

Donation fund:
Balance, June 30, 1925	117.54
Receipts, including interest	298.33
Total desk and donation fund receipts	15,882.02
Total receipts	253,451.62

EXPENDITURES

Central library and branches:
Salaries (exclusive of bindery)	$178,363.26
Books	43,039.70
Postage	1,070.00
Subscriptions to periodicals	2,530.52
Printing annual report	99.60
Membership fees in learned societies	122.08
Binding services	7,480.10
Binding supplies	696.50
Binding (outside work)	1,823.40
Contingent expenses	15,949.20
Dodge car upkeep	181.36
Total expenditures	251,355.72
Balance, desk and donation funds	2,095.90
	253,451.62

AUDIT BY FINANCE COMMITTEE OF LIBRARY TRUSTEES

We, the finance committee of the board of library trustees, hereby certify that we have had the accounts of the treasurer of the board audited, so far as the same relate to the desk and the donation funds, including the Henry Pastor memorial fund, the Women's Anthropological Society fund, and the vending-machine fund, receipts and disbursements, and find that all the receipts have been collected and accounted for; that the disbursements are represented by canceled checks and vouchers, and that the same are correct. We also certify that the balances shown by the report of the treasurer correspond to the balances in bank.

                                        C. J. BELL, *Chairman*,
                                        JOHN B. LARNER,
                                                Finance Committee.

WASHINGTON, D. C., *August 20, 1926.*

This is to certify that I have audited the desk-fund and donation-fund accounts of the Public Library and find that there was on hand in the desk-fund account on the 1st day of July, 1925, the sum of $378.36; that the receipts during the year ended June 30, 1926, amounted to the sum of $15,087.79, and that the expenditures for the same period amounted to the sum of $13,588.76, leaving a balance in the hands of the treasurer as of June 30, 1926, of $1,877.39, which amount is shown to be on deposit in bank after allowance for outstanding checks.

I find that the balance on hand July 1, 1925, in the donation-fund account was $117.54, and that the receipts during the year amounted to the sum of $298.33, and that the balance on hand as of June 30, 1926, amounted to the sum of $218.51.

Respectfully submitted.

A. S. VIPOND, *Auditor.*

SUMMARY OF ESTIMATES, 1928

Congressional appropriation, 1927	$271,300
Estimated desk fund, 1927	15,878
Total available funds, 1927	287,178
Estimates, 1928	396,260
Increase over congressional appropriation	124,960
Increase over congressional appropriation plus desk fund	109,082

This increase of $124,960 over congressional appropriation for 1927 represents:

(1) For present establishment—

Central library and overhead	$17,700	
Branches, Takoma, Southeast, Mount Pleasant, and Chevy Chase-Tenley	13,460	
Increments (1 each)	7,400	
Total		$38,560

(2) For new projects—

Eight new school branches	62,250	
Rhode Island Avenue branch	9,150	
Site for northeast branch library	15,000	
Total		86,400

LIBRARY LAW, AS AMENDED

[PUBLIC—No. 85—69TH CONGRESS]

An act to amend the act approved June 3, 1896, entitled "An act to establish and provide for the maintenance of a free public library and reading room in the District of Columbia."

Be it enacted by the Senate and House of Representatives of the United States of America in Congress assembled, That the act approved June 3, 1896, entitled "An act to establish and provide for the maintenance of a free public library and reading room in the District of Columbia," be, and the same is hereby, amended so as to read as follows:

"SECTION 1. That a free public library is hereby established and shall be maintained in the District of Columbia, which shall be the property of the said District and a supplement of the public educational system of said District. Said library shall consist of a central library and such number of branch libraries so located and so supported as to furnish books and other printed matter and information service convenient to the homes and offices of all residents of the said District. All actions relating to such library, or for the recovery of any penalties lawfully established in relation thereto, shall be brought in the name of the District of Columbia, and the Commissioners of the said District are authorized on behalf of said District to accept and take title to all gifts, bequests, and devises for the purpose of aiding in the maintenance or endowment of said library; and the Commissioners of said District are further authorized to receive, as component parts of said library, collections of books and other publications that may be transferred to them.

"SEC. 2. That in order to make the said library an effective supplement of the public educational system of the said District and to furnish the system of branch libraries provided for in section 1 hereof, the board of library trustees, hereinafter provided, is authorized to enter into agreements with the Board of Education of the said District for the establishment and maintenance of branch libraries in suitable rooms in such public-school buildings of the said District as will supplement the central library and branch libraries in separate buildings. The board of library trustees, hereinafter provided, is authorized within the limits of appropriations first made therefor, to rent suitable buildings or parts of buildings for use as branch libraries and distributing stations.

"SEC. 3. That all persons who are permanent or temporary residents of the District of Columbia shall be entitled to the privileges of said library, including the use of the books contained therein, as a lending or circulating library, subject to such rules and regulations as may be lawfully established in relation thereto. Persons living outside of the said District, but having regular business or employment or attending school in the said District, shall for the purpose of this act be deemed temporary residents. Other persons residing in counties of Maryland and Virginia adjacent to the said District may gain the privilege of withdrawing books from the said library by the payment of fees fixed by the board of library trustees hereinafter provided. After June 30, 1927, all fees shall be paid weekly to the collector of taxes of the District of Columbia for deposit in the Treasury of the United States to the credit of said District of Columbia.

"SEC. 4. That the said library shall be in charge of a board of library trustees, who shall purchase the books, magazines, and newspapers and procure the necessary appendages for such library. The said board of trustees shall be composed of nine members, each of whom shall be a taxpayer in the District of Columbia and shall serve without compensation. They shall be appointed by the Commissioners of the District of Columbia and shall hold office for six years: *Provided,* That at the first meeting of the said board the members shall be divided by lot into three classes. The first class, composed of three members, shall hold office for two years; the second class, composed of three members, shall hold office for four years; the third class, composed of three members, shall hold office for six years. Any vacancy occurring in said board shall be filled by the District Commissioners. Said board shall have power to provide such regulations for its organization and government as it may deem necessary.

"SEC. 5. That the said board shall have power to provide for the proper care and preservation of said library, to prescribe rules for taking and returning books, to fix, assess, and collect fines and penalties for the loss of or injury to books, and for the retention of books beyond the period fixed by library regulations, and to establish all other needful rules and regulations for the management of the library as the said board shall deem proper. All fines and penalties so collected shall, after June 30, 1927, be paid weekly to the collector of taxes of the District of Columbia for deposit in the Treasury of the United States to the credit of said District of Columbia. The said board of trustees shall appoint a librarian to have the care and superintendence of said library, who shall be responsible to the board of trustees for the impartial enforcement of all rules and regulations lawfully established in relation to said library. The said librarian shall appoint such assistants as the board shall deem necessary to the proper conduct of the library. The said board of library trustees shall make an annual report to the Commissioners of the District of Columbia relative to the management of the said library.

"SEC. 6. That said Commissioners of the said District are authorized to include in their annual estimates for appropriations such sums as they may deem necessary for the proper maintenance of said library, including branches, for the purchase of land for sites for library buildings, and for the erection and enlargement of necessary library buildings."

Approved, April 1, 1926.

LAW AFFECTING BRANCH LIBRARY SITES

Extract from National Capital Park and Planning Commission law (Public 158, approved April 30, 1926) relating to library sites:

"(b) That the said commission is hereby charged with the duty of preparing, developing, and maintaining a comprehensive, consistent, and coordinated plan for the National Capital and its environs, which plan shall include recommendations to the proper executive authorities as to traffic and transportation; plats and subdivisions; highways, parks, and parkways; school and library sites; playgrounds; drainage, sewerage, and water supply; housing, building, and zoning regulations; public and private buildings; bridges and water fronts; commerce and industry; and other proper elements of city and regional planning."

NATIONAL VERSUS LOCAL LIBRARY

LIBRARY OF CONGRESS,
Washington, December 11, 1925.

MY DEAR DOCTOR BOWERMAN: I have been looking over your latest report and, in connection with the needs that it states, have been reviewing your report of 1924. I am confirmed in my previous belief that, within the means at your disposal, your library is doing, with enthusiasm and the very best directing intelligence, as creditable work as is being done by any municipal library in the United States, but I am impressed anew with the inadequacy of your resources. For over 20 years I have watched your efforts to enlarge these; and I notice that invariably they are hampered by an impression in the appropriation committees that, with the Library of Congress available, much less in the way of facilities is required from the library of the District than is expected of the ordinary municipal library elsewhere.

This is, of course, most unfortunate and is based on a misconception. Except as regards the Members of Congress themselves and their families (for whom the Library of Congress is "all kinds of a library"), the Library of Congress is for residents of the District purely a reference library; the only loans of books which it makes outside of the official use being to a few persons engaged in very special research requiring books not ordinarily to be found in a municipal library. This leaves to the library of the District, besides a considerable amount of ordinary reference use which its location conveniences, the entire outside service to (1) the general reader, (2) the schools and the ordinary student; and with a population of the character of that of Washington the needs of these groups are such as require and justify facilities equal to those of any municipal library in a city of a half million people.

They can be met (1) only by a more ample collection in your central building, with a staff more highly equipped from a professional standpoint; (2) by additional branch libraries and delivery stations; and (3) by branch collections in the public schools. In other words, an organization as complete as that which has become standard in other cities.

And the existence of the Library of Congress, with the facilities that it accords, no more relieves the necessity for such an organization than the existence of three great reference libraries in Chicago relieves the public library there.

I wish, indeed, that this distinction could become clear to the appropriation committees, and that you will succeed in convincing them that the services of the two libraries, though slightly overlapping in one respect, are in general quite distinct. In point of fact, what the general public of Washington gets from the Library of Congress, so far from being a substitute for the service of a public library, stimulates interests to which only a public lending library can respond.

Very sincerely yours,

HERBERT PUTNAM, *Librarian.*

Dr. GEORGE F. BOWERMAN, *Librarian.*
The Public Library of the District of Columbia, Washington, D. C.

CPSIA information can be obtained
at www.ICGtesting.com
Printed in the USA
BVHW04*1055170918
527708BV00015B/2254/P